Engineering a Love Story

Andrew Haber, a Man of the 21st Century
(Should Be Charge for Gravity)

Pamela Morgan

Order this book online at www.trafford.com
or email orders@trafford.com

Most Trafford titles are also available at major online book retailers.

Print information available on the last page.

ISBN: 978-1-4907-5670-7 (sc)
         978-1-4907-5669-1 (e)

Our mission is to efficiently provide the world's finest, most comprehensive book publishing service, enabling every author to experience
success. To find out how to publish your book, your way, and have it available worldwide, visit us online at www.trafford.com

Any people depicted in stock imagery provided by Thinkstock are models,
and such images are being used for illustrative purposes only.
Certain stock imagery © Thinkstock.

Trafford rev. 03/11/2015

www.trafford.com

North America & international
toll-free: 1 888 232 4444 (USA & Canada)
fax: 812 355 4082

Andy Haber. He came to the cold barren moon and I love him.

An awkward start. We met - say sometime during the course of three years at one of our just "Hi" or "Hello" episodes. He stood near me as I sat on a high stool. The name of the restaurant was Mombasa Bay and the gathering was the SSSF club. Sailing Singles of South Florida. An elite and friendly hunting ground for captains and crew. The resataurant is out of business yet presently we return to the area to patronize Taverna Ora - a Greek restaurant where Andy and I have been known to dance on their tables. Solid, sacred ground.

At the beginning as now, Andy lets his beard grow long. Cute, but a little disgustng at first, I could see Andy at first lean up to the bar counter and kind of soak up some beer in it.

Ironically he doesn't like beer and won't drink alcohol. He has had the beard since high school. But it is soft and manly and cute. And no, he doesn't carry his dinner around in it.

Andy's best feature was hidden from me for years until he said something about us sailing while looking into my eyes with his brown and ember eyes reflecting burning charcoal. I had never seen anything so beautiful!

"Are you seeing all right?" I said.

"Yeah. Why?"

"You are showing dark mosaic eyes with a cave like fire!"

"Oh."

"No." He looked away. And a caring look. He strokes his beard.

It was wintertime but here in Fort Lauderdale that doesn't matter. We had been through our meeting stage after we found out where each other of us was from - both from PA - the hardest city for people to leave because they can't get the gas money -and he looked at me and said:

"This probably doesn't mean much to you but a magazine at work has a cold sniffling cow on its cover."

Andy let me know who he wanted. His way of saying he was attracted to me was the same as saying he couldn't find any good women. Surely he didn't mean me! Eventually through all of the years of "Hi" and "Hello" I asked him if I could compete to qualify as a good single woman. He told me he was short on time for me. What does he do?

Soon I found he was dating Carol Atkinson, a petite smart woman who is also a lawyer. She let me know he was too much for her and etc. "You've seen the size of his hands! (Big)"

How did she know what I thought that means? (The way to measure a guy's endowmant). That, I wasn't interested in yet but it was good to know. It seemed that like in a while I'd be blessed with the proof and I would wait forever for that!

By the way, within a few years, Carol found another one there and sailed to the Virgin Island to wed. Andy and I would wait.

Meanwhile, there were more people pairing Andy and me up. "You see that gut over there?" a French sailor motioned to Andy. "He is yours!"

Oh my God. I waited. "But he may be too good for you."

I began to choke up. That was one time I knew I had to have him. Next, I had to find out more from the sailors about Andy. And, not surprisingly so I found out a resounding "He's a good guy?"

The women's room was always crowded at these sailor parties. I tried to may out my territory. And, I was serious. The new women with too much prostitute makeup had to put in their places. That came easy to me. "This is no place for whores." And, "These men are good marriage material. You don't come here to whore around!" A few of the women I'd never see again and that's okay. I rmember an adage:

"Men can tell the difference between precious metals and common ores!"

A tacit agreement between us is I clean house and this is okay because I get closer to finding out about this genious. Dust always accumulates, floors always need polishing and vacuuming, dishes done and toussled beds made. I find interesting toys from a solar powered toy car to an antique 1969 MG car in the garage over to a load of books and magazines.

He is on top of everything and he lectures to me telling me who makes what car from what where and how much. Andy is a floating factory.

He owns and drives a car selected by yours truly. This shows I am in his heart. What will be our next car during this time of transition and energy shortage?

Early on Andy finds out I love to travel. After we established boredom together we decided we love being together and discussing our different experiences. All couples can unite here. We are growing, moving and having fun together like that.

With my sister Marilyn Dixon as chaperone we began with a weekend at Disneyworld. For those of you who know, that is a lovely place to learn. Andy and I do all of the educational games there and wonder and wander. It is a great soul sealant. Meanwhile, we were establishing levels of trust. Already I knew I see him every Thursday night at the SSSF party. He never missed that. But most importantly he spoke from his heart to me. He discusses money and investments with me and together we are frugal.

And, we travelled more with Big Sis Marilyn. The Florida Keys are great. For car music we like Celine Dion and Swing Out Sister. And soon on our own Andy and I began Caribbean cruising going to the Bahamas, Mexico and Belize (to the horror to some friends who think genious engineers don't know how to handle themselves diplomaticly far away).

And I too am an engineer. A female engineer trained at Cornell University. I know. Ugh. I too had been bitten by the bug. Math has always come easily to me. You can tell verbal hasn't here. Ha. What can I tell you? I was on scholarship. I was known as the girl you turn upside down to use as a mop. Me. A mop! With my blonde locks!

But ironicly, if I had selected to attend RPI (Andy's alma mater) I could have known him sooner. Yeah, he said. But he certainly didn't go to RPI to find a wife! All men tease like that.

I tell him we would've made many beautiful babies if only...He blushes.

Andy and I are the same horoscope sign Capricorn - an earth sign. Perhaps that is why I have no trouble with the earth. But water, fire and wind have brought havoc.

I held an apartment in Deerfield Beach beginning in 1990. In 2002 water pipes in the bathroom burst and flooded the apartment, so I moved to a third floor apartment two buildings away part of a four building complex. The location was great being walking distance to restaurants, supermarket, department store and even a dollar store. Andy helped me to move all in the interest of keeping two places for Andy and me. I really didn't want to move, having lived there twelve years, but the manager recommended the new apartment for the same low rate because it would provide a patio balcony for my parakeet "France". "France" is my new millenium baby bird with black, white and blue feathers. She is with me today on her eighth birdday, uh, birthday. And I love her.

Four years into living in the new apartment wind gusts from Hurricane Wilma took off the roof and dropped three inches of water in the midst of the night. I survived by keeping my bird, a transistor radio and bottled water with me in a closet for fifteen hours. Andy's house was unharmed. Yet I stuck it out there to see a new roof addition.

The final blow to our independence came on September 30, 2007 when a huge chemical explosion engulfed the building of my last residence five o'clock in the morning and six months from my grandmother Mimi's birthday. My aunt Louise says that is something good.

But, all of the buildings had the same tenuous natural gas pipes. I then called Andy on the phone and tore over to his house in our 2005 Hyundai Accent with my important papers and bird France. I begged to move in with him and he said "Yes". Thank Jesus. Thank Andy. This is insight to a great man.

Often I reminisce about the "Thunderball Apartments". Andy saw me through it all. Where I am now with him I have a cooling swimming pool and good a/c.

Andy saved my life. And I am finding out he has done much good elsewheres too.

For instance yesterday he buzz sawed, glued and screwed together a new mailbox!

At some date, I can't remember when, I told Andy that he had to be a machine for me. Flesh and blood are too weak for me. He paniced like a true humanist at heart. (I feel this) But maybe he is fooling me.

For example I told him I am everything from a trash compactor (jumping on trash bags) to even, yes, being a love machine at times. My previous boyfriend claimed to be a piston engine. (pretty good, no?)

Andy mumbled something about being a computer. Soon I'll ask him again. The thought doesn't much interest him, though. And I continue to imbue his body with lotion and good loving, in that order.

And next, cave men. Yes. Cave men. I started in on this. Just look out the window and see all the cars move on wheels. The cave man is still around! Andy thinks this is funny too and a few days later said he presented this concept at work and told them: "If only the cave man had a patent. He'd be a trillionaire!!!"

Last week we bought a new parakeet birdie for $15.99. The cashier typed in our names and address so the State of Florida could know it's home.

The baby bird is too young to know its gender. Six weeks. She will be good company to our older bird. We gave our older bird "France" a partner and buddy "Jesse".

"Jesse" is Andy's middle name. She/he has very recessive coloring. Grayish, lilacish and bluish. For now, at least, she/he is quiet and shy. Kind of like us.

Andy said thay are my birds. I tell him that he couldn't be more involved! He paid for the bird, gave his address as its home, drove to the store, pays for the bird seed, calcium, cuttle bone, gravel paper, mineral treat, toys and tolerates all. For sure he is the dad! He smiles and goes upstairs.

When there might breakout a fight from friction he goes upstairs where his four workrooms are and I sit downstairs with the birds. Other times it is west or east wings here.

Kinda like garage/house for many couples. And on Sundays: in the house/ outside the house doing yard work. And on other days: laundry/ cleanup. And, anything at all/ blonde hair care.

Two cars race through our human bodies. Red and white synonymous blood cells. They pump and give us energy.

And what does the future hold for us? Electric cars producing a cup of water for us or corn bio fuels we can pop for popcorn as we drive along. Will we need to go as far in the new cars as futuristic cities develope? Family bicycles again?

And where will we live and vacation in the future? Same? or perhaps something like the hover hotel. Step inside and the place moves for your weight? Outer space life? Immaculate life?

How does this come to us? Andy and I have spent years developing theories of coincidence. A lousy example is driving along in our car with a restaurant ad on the radio news and seeing the same restaurant on the corner there. A better example is similar birthdays. Numerology is always good to use. And of course similar likes (food) and dislikes (perverseness).

For years there was no end to our coincidences. We laugh and call them co-inky-dinkys! Winky Dinkey anyone?

Andy's exact number of cassette tapes fit well into a designer bag of mine. He and I both like animals. (I say he has beautiful animal eyes) He holds onto old space and rocketry magazines and I hold some family antiques from the nineteenth century, i.e. jewelry, lamps and a Winsor rocking chair from one of my Presidential ancestors. The list goes on.

Will futuristic energy cars pump red and white for us? Will they be entertainment centers and moving cup holder we love now?

Andy had a trains set too for use under a Christmas tree. Will we have super electric magnetic trains in our future? Airplanes. Is there enough air space?

Population-wise Andy and I figured as many people in South Florida as threads in the living room shag rug! OK

Which brings me to a universal truth. Engineers are the measure of how great a society is. There have always been doctors and lawyers in every society to help people feel better and to move money around but it is the engineers who create great nations. We even go to the moon because of engineers. The moon is barren, yes, but what could we do with a hose and bucket up there? Think about it. I am excited by the thought. Hover hotels on the moon for weekend vacations and holidays.

OK. We have touched the moon-rock at the NASA Space center and we lived well. We have seen the moon buggy and it could be made to be more comfortable all right.

Golf anyone?

Andy wears and owns only two pairs of shoes. Work/dress and sneakers. I have many pairs.

We shop for his clothing together and it's cheap. Alterations on the pant legs cost more than the pants!

I like him wearing white shirts, more expensive ones, partly because I sewed men's white shirts in a factory before going to college. That way I feel appreciation and the money was good.

Andy came to Fort Lauderdale directly out of RPI University in Troy, New York, to work. Over fifteen years he developed a new phone system. Bravo. I came annually to visit my sister Marilyn and her husband John who were both working. Soon I would make my residence here after I spent time in Europe trying to get three previous novels published. Meanwhile Andy was working and buying a house. Presently our space capsule.

He talks much about the process of buying the house and recalls spending days in the sales office bidding and waiting to be checked out. Apparantly there were three bids on this property and by fluke his bid won. He works hard for his money and knows how t spend it.

Immediately he covered all windows with good blinds for the light. The plush green carpet is good. The house is supposed to be the builder's house but he was selling out. I see the house across the street in this developement is tilted. At the end of his life Andy has expressed the wish to sell the house to anyone but a family. Any guess why?

Neither Andy nor me have been inculcated (taught) anything about having babies and raising children so we no longer pretend to. We are fun loving adults and that is OK. He knows I am childless and still comes to me. The moon.

October 26, 2008. Overnight our bird "France" died. She was covered overnight with a black jersey, she was suffering and wimpering, and when I uncovered her the next morning rigor mordis had set in. We loved the bird and she is in our hearts. Now she is in bird heaven.

Andy and I are close and mingling. A few weeks ago he said he was going to get his hair cut and I got my hair cut. I told him I needed a new wallet and he got a new wallet.

And so it goes on. You might think my thoughts ar a bit scattered but there is always something else going on at the same time. No?

We search for energy solutions.

It's always beautiful weather here in Fort Lauderdale and if you go to the beach it's always something. To preserve it, the beach has been rebuilt from more rocks and sand to a much used fishing peer. Andy and I started with kite flying. After 5 pm the life guards go home and it is a good time to fly a kite and watch the nuances of the sunset. With no help we flew and reeled in a kite. We discussed scientists making electricity from a spark. Then we rolled in the sand and kissed to celebrate life and gratitude that electricity had been done. KISS.

Also, we take time to stroll along the beach. We have a favorite place to visit i.e. beach decks hosted by newlyweds and their guests. We are happy by the sight. I know Andy is the one and like all the rest not until death do us part.

And back to the scientific discoveries. Andy wants to know how all the engineering measurements get their names. He knows F is for farad and measures capacitance. Ampere is named for a Frenchman named Andre Marie Ampere. Ohm is named for Georg Simon Ohm, a German. Volt is named for Alessandro Volta, an Italian. Why?

I wander in my thoughts to our new little bird named for Andy's middle name. I impress him. I named life for him. Jesse. Just Jesse. One bird energy.

Andy has always hung on the right, heterosexual willing and unwilling and on the left gay or shy.

Once a week.

At the beginning I told him, quote, I don't want you chauffeuring a dick to me. And that made a difference. We had been engaged 2½ years before I could bolster that up. And that wasn't enough. Neither were his kidney stones surgeries.

And than, one evening out of happenstance, I heard a drum roll (similar to the old church bells in one's ear) that made it feel like time had demanded Andy and me be together.

That came soon after making measurements to the moon together. Anyway, Andy said that guys at work had some of that too. Eventually screwing - the engineering term for making love or hanky panky - became practiced.

My starting request was once a week, everything else the same. Like other so called couples. And that meant once during the weeknights. Only one problem. The guys at his work said he was unpredictably different during the week because of it. They asked us to confine our screwing to the weekend! Ha!

We have a new baby bird and Andy came to the barren moon. The a/c is cooler and the train is almost here again. He works hard and has an interview card with a MIC company. He just got his hair cut and some gray removal so he thinks he is pretty cool.

He liked my father and thinks he could possibly be the only good one but acquiesces. So many people ask him how he becomes such a good engineer and to dismiss that silly question he says both his parents were alcoholics and that is how they dealt with their problems. Also, a funnier rational is that his mother smoked for more that fifty years!

We have wobbled into recession. The bird and I don't need much food. We have seen over one hundred theatre movies mostly followed by dinner at a restaurant. Andy is quiet when he eats and always leaves a neat plate.

I wonder about hormones. There is a full moon shortly. My mood waxes and wanes. Good and bad vibes.

I am getting wrinkly and he says not to do that! My Aunt Kay and Uncle Don say quizzically "Babies are born with alot of wrinkles and that smooth, don't they?"

Andrew near moon rover

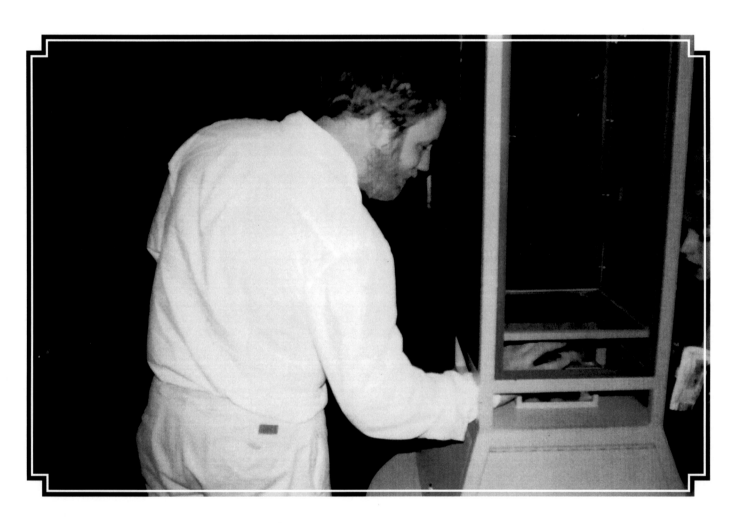

Andrew feels moon rock @ NASA Kennedy Space Center

Pam feels moon rock @ NASA Kennedy Space Center

Andy and Pam in Disney

Andy never modelled but he thinks that I have is neat. We constantly need pictures of ourselves and our environment. I have a simulated moon and buggy background picture and I love us touching the moon rock at NASA Kennedy space center! And, oh, by the way, the name Kennedy is one of his family names on his mother's bramch.

Privately I have been studying ancient Egyptian art and have the feeling people 2000 years plus will still be interested in leaders such as King Tut and Nefertiti. I am pretty sure Andy sneaks a peak at the Bible and everyone believes that study will last forever too.

Anyway, this space capsule house that we live in needs repair. The air conditioning leaks and is wetting the ceiling and floors. That is something they know all about in the space shuttle with multi-layered doors to the outside unknown. Parallel? So, to pretty it up here we brought trees indoors and put on Christmas lights. And as a special treat Andy put an electric train with 21 compartment cars on it around our pine (fake) tree. If you can't fake it how can it ever be real? We enhance that with scented pine candles. Not bad, eh?

Tonights food is in the fridge and just needs a dish and microwave shot. Andy and I are just at the point of my selecting the menu for our dinners every night instead of getting his approval. I do not want to disappoint him. I chide that even Einstein put a tip under his dinner plate for the waitress his wife.

And so I continue to carry on in the kitchen with two or three meals at restaurants each week. And there we get our pictures taken too. We laugh about how we should list what we eat there too so we can see our corresponding health. We have hundreds of beautiful pictures from the many beautiful restaurants here in Fort Lauderdale, without the nagging clean up. We save money on not cleaning up at home and ordering food at nearly the cost for what we receive at the supermarkets.

Right now I go on break to do laundry. It is our own thing. Andy and I do our own laundries and as his payoff for his extra work, he is the bread winner, I make special of my blonde hair. The blonde clean and soft angel hair adorning on my shoulders and head.

Enough you say? Have I been identified as another ditsy, wispy blonde? Read on! I truly am fool of interesting foo foo.

Debarking from the Majesty of the Seas, 12-26-2008, we found a beautiful Ardasta zoo in the center of the Bahamas and Andy and I took video pictures. Flamingos, parakeets, big cats and bob cats are here in Paradise. We stayed one hour and then back to the van.

Andy would make a good ambassador because foreigners like him and he is diplomatic. The Germans and Asians made a good presence on this cruise this time. He had his way. And by now I have learned that he is always right.

Our trip to Miami's port by stretch limo was amazing. First timers we looked around in awe and played the radio music. We arrived early and got on board to go to an orientation class which Andy called a "shopping thing". Next we mustered for safety lessons followed by a lamb dinner with rosemary and Andy had an Atlantic cod dinner.

We unpacked and Andy filled the closet with his tuxedo. Our cabin attendant brought ice and that started a soda bill for twenty-four dollars for three days! And too, our travel agent delivered a wine bottle with all sorts of warnings on it to our stateroom. This we left behind.

Waking up at 8 am to a phone call it was up and out to the Windjammer cafe and then debarking to a private Bahamian island called CoCoCay Island. We soon found contentment in two separate hammocks so we could sleep.

Once roused, we completed a mile long nature walk and returned along the calm and smooth ocean. We viewed all sights from a trampoline on the ocean to a family eating bananas together. Returning to the ship's gangplank our identification was checked and we boarded. No stamping yet.

Andy looked superb in a white tie tux. I added a hair piece with my formal dress. We have pictures from this.

Unfortunately the following day I had sea sickness. Made it to the room where I changed into a looser fitting dress. My God. The next day I heard my Jap friend Yugo also had seasickness. Rough weather.

Andy drew the attention of Yugo and Kiko, travelling Japanese partners, at our dinner table for six aboard ship. Little Yugo flirted by pampering and patting her belly and tossing her hair back to expose an unusual black hairline. Hair that could be no other color.

"Blonde hair is for Halloween," she said. Her only concession was "Red hair is the worst!"

We continued discussing video arcade games, laughed, and left it at that. We bought our cruise pictures and made it home safely.

Andy has begun to dazzle me with sparkling conversation. Morning and night. He reads alot, more than ten magazines each month, and likes to pass some of the information along to me. He knows I like that. When we first started living together I would say that I needed some knowledge to keep in my mind upstairs. Ever since that he has been feeding info to me. I have insatiable questions.

Andy's education has been a life long journey, so he says. All engineering. His smarts, he says, come from his mother who attended Vassar, a prestigeous Seven Sister school. This is how he ingratiated himself to me, after he heard that I am an Ivy Leaguer. I had tried to hide this fact realizing men don't want intelligent women. I had a guilt-free three years like that as some blonde bimbo.

I cajole him saying he thought an education was good for women, but only if she was maternal too.

My father predicted all of this too thinking there might be a man out there who wants an intelligent woman! Rah daddy and Andy!

Of course game playing came with the territory. And there is no end becoming a blonde war game toyer. Many men only seem to want to play war games with you. Unfortunately that almost destroys my sane easy society completely. Well well.

Andy's mother played a key role in his education. His father too. Both wanted to see their son attend college. Once Andy could read books he was set. He knows everything about everything and there is no stopping him. He doesn't mark up or dog ear his books and he claims he can go into any book in his library and find a specific written detail. Pretty amazing! Getting Andy through high school was easy with all high scores and good grades. He advanced to RPI in Troy, N.Y..

There, he found a same sex fantasy world which made him into the man he is today. He refers back to a dorm room encounter with football players storming doors and windows and desks for sex. There wasn't enough of that he said. Needless to say, the football season finished 0-13 his frosh year. Eventually Andy would learn to live more independantly.

Once again, it is always amazing to me how I missed seeing Andy in math class and others because I attended Cornell U. on engineering scholarship. We are just a couple of years apart and I too had been accepted to RPI.

Such is fate playing for us to meet later rather than sooner!

Andy has an MG '69 car in the garage with no floor board or speed. The chassis needs polishing. It might be fit for a lithium battery "engine" in the glove compartment. He is game. I feel that is for the next generation's American vehickle. Back to that later.

Now, Andy wants solar power panels on the house to replace FPL power company but we haven't heard any complaints about that yet. Thunder, lightening and tree and bird droppings could cause a problem with a roof study enough for any type of weather. This month is January, 2009 and our two Christmas trees are lit. Soon too a Valentine tree? Perhaps a nesting place for two parakeets?

By the way, Jesse was on Andy's "finger perch" Inauguration day, wecoming Michelle and Barach Obama. Such a celebration for us!

The bird hides behind chairs and climbs cable wire. It's a "he" all right. "France" the bird lives on in my memory since 2000 Common Era strongly. Soon "Jesse" will show his own integrity and important identity. There. Add one colossal note that no matter what, thus far, Jesse doesn't bite! Now he sings some more. I go to work on our 2005 Hyundai Accent's fluids. I have been gyped of antifreeze at the car dealer. Why do all of my cars have radiator problems? That, my friend I must nip in the bud. Would electric cars have fewer maintanence problems?

Meanwhile I muse on even more diamond jewelery. My very own setting and design. Hooray!

And now Andy's next problem is to get a power box for the sprinkler system. Our lawn looks like a desert.

And, we need new blue jeans. His are filthy from pressure cleaning theroof of the garage and house and suffer from overall wear.

And too, we need new calendars that too show the mmmmoons cycle. There I go again! Do do do do.

Yesterday was a square root day: 3/3/09! Andy and I celebrated by going to the restaurant Taverna Ora. There we celebrated with golden gauze belly dancing on tables. And too by noticing a new tendency of mine of noting the food we eat when we are out. Here we had North Pacific salmon, rice and spinach; all spiced and garnered. To top it off with coca cola and 7 UP beverages.

For the first time Andy ordered the same food as me. And he has started at home to eat from my bag of frankfurters. I discovered he is a bun and mustard kind of guy.

After discussing buying new furniture we ended up cleaning and rearranging what we have in the living room. The bird has a tree house now with a cage and stand near a six foot tall silk tree. We have not yet given him a second cage but we have one for him.

The Christmas trees are still "up" and slowly we are opening all of the gifts there were lingering under the tree. Food gifts of candy and pretzels.

I need a new chair in the bedroom. I currently use a bar stool of Andy's creation. I want a big new jewelry box. A desk would be nice. These are all things Andy could craft but he is too busy at work now. And his night school course on woodworking has been cancelled.

Tonight we play tennin in Floridas version of winter cold with Marilyn. It's good. We too are planning a Disneyworld venue with a holiday in Asia when I turn sixty and Andy is fifty-eight. Why not? We have been to Mexico in 2004 and that was a fun cruise and bus ride. Or, London again would be good…a place to find retirement monestaries. Places where flowers are cultivated and books are read in a deep pure quiet. We'll see. All I want to know is that I am not alone with life. I love Andy. He is my best friend. I count blessings.

I purchased a 52 inch wide high definition TV and stand and surge protector and cleaner plus cable COMCAST. Its fabulous and Andy will admit that.

We often play tennis Wednesday night with my sister Marilyn and come home at nine to watch Mythbusters (science show). My favorite piece is the golf ball version car. It has great aeorodynamics! The "dimpled car" saves 10% gas volume. Hail science! Will we see that in the future in fruition? What will it be made of? Plastic cars? Gluable dimpled mats to be placed on car bodies to save energy?

Life goes on and next Andy rented a pressure cleaner for driveway and rooftop for seventy dollars a day. I take water to him for half hour water breaks.

Soon, Andy is back to practicing and producing woodworking projects. His mentor friend Sam Burton is a hoot. Sam runs evening woodworking class in a high school. The tables and gadgets Andy makes are amazing. Recently he designed and made a new wooden mail box!

Mut and Jeff? Tom and Jerry? No! Better and more clever. Andy etched numbers and painted the mail box! What is next for that genius Andy! But why does all of his blondwood get painted brown?

When Andy is not working he is working. Another two bookshelves are assembled. I try to neatly stack his magazines on the shelves. IEEE, Science News, Nuts and Volts, Aviation Week and RPI magazines to name a few!

And this turns me to green energy for the house? Solar powered batteries? longer lasting lightbulbs and wind energy soon here? That is something of the future.

Our air conditioning was loud and inefficient. He bought a new air conditioner and paid $3,800 including a FPL deduction. Andy wants to know why no one asked him where he got the money! We have a 2020 year warrenty!

Andy thinks sex is ridiculous. Even though he is good at it. His kiss is delicious and his touch is divine. And, as I thought, there is no stopping us after we get started. We go all the way! The key is when he says he is tired. Or, when he starts scratching his skin to let me know it is dry and he needs a moisturising massage. That is a good trick.

My clue is to play some mood music. Oh, the royalties the music industry could make if they only knew and could!

Cryptically Andy said, "If I had known sex was so great we wouldn't have bought the house first!" Go figure. Where does that leave his two time shares?

Recently we resided in his Delray Beach, Florida time share resort for one week in October, 2009. I made a ten minute movie there for us to remember. It was windy but we managed. On film I lost a shoe in the ocean. Good for Americas Home Videos. Anyways, my point is now that we make a good looking couple. He just has to cut his beard down sometimes!

Back to reality. If Andy doesn't sleep after a good time with sex he might be a little goofy at work the next day. This is why we do hanky panky on weekends. Otherwise He complained that noone at work is any fun. Who knows when he is roused and why? What? I must explore his fantasy sex life more.

I help to bring Christmas time to the Habers. Andy's family doesn't really celebrate this holiday and I think the reason is atheism. On exception there is sometimes a card.

This year, 2009, we have three Christmas parties to attend. One on Christmas eve with my sister Marilyn where we open presents under an artificial six foot tall tree lighted and decorated. We light a pine scented candle for effect.

Another with the Mensa group at a private house, this time in Hollywood where we prayed and dined and then participated in making tree ornaments we could then bring home!

A third Christmas party in January at a swank Fort Lauderdale restaurant named "Sage", a new American cafe, with the docent volunteer group with the Fort Lauderdale Museum of Art. The docents were very welcoming and everyone was going somewhere else! That's interesting.

After all of this fantabulous hullaballoo we return to another reality and read that NASA is closing. Boo hoo. Alot of dreams down the tubes. The salvation is that we are beafing up the space station. Hopefully we can have safely manned lift off and re-entry missions that won't jeapardise life!

And, we can still touch the moon rock and decide if it is worth mining new materials. Now, that is exciting!

Andy the domineering.

"Can't go to work hot!"

He claims that the water bed is too hot. He left me in the middle of the night for the guest room bed. Coyly I said: "You won't sleep without me!"

Well, the bed cooled down and he came to me a few hours later all cuddly. I mumbled something about talking to my mother then and cried. He didn't see me cry. That happened on the eve of Martin Luther King's birthday.

The following night when we sat at home watching telle the water heater banged and popped! Water began flooding the house. Thanks to quick thinking and he turned off the water supply outside. Yikes.

In less than forty eight hours, I don't know why that number, I had that fixed. Andy the provider paid for it. Relief. And I knew who to call for help. Maureen - just a girlfriend! Anywho, we weren't supposed to be home then. The house would've flooded. We were supposed to play volleyball with the Coconut Creek Community. Thank god for playing hookie on a holiday. Will I get a big bonus with Andy.

Thanks to Andy his storage of big water bottles came in handy for personal and bathroom usage for those in between hours. I see why he does some of those things. That's Andy the provider. If we needed it we could fill the bottles with pool water. Done with a six year warranty for nine hundred and ninety three dollars.

Volleyball remains fun. Even though we have played and lost three times now. Get the serve in and try to return the ball. And guess what? Andy lost his wedding band at the court. I had to call Bruno the coordinator to pull out the metal detector to find it after two days searching. The ring was returned to Andy and we were all happy. I hope.

Today is Easter Sundat time 2010! Andy's small family stayed with us here from Monday thru Friday. They wound up taking a talking Easter bunny home

Andy had selected from the store. And, we had a busy fun jammed up weekend for them for one week. For one, M V & L (Martin, Valerie and Lya Haber) visited the safari in WPB unfortunately with no a/c in their silver Honda SUV. Uh oh.

Two, the five of us had a picnic at our local pavillion followed by a barefoot tennis game with only Andy in his street shoes! Three, we dined followed by a dinner show at the Mai Kai - a well known Polynesian restaurant with a garden, picture ops and fire dancing keeping us busy for three hours for a sum totalling 336 dollars!

And Marilyn, my sister, joined us there. She was appropriate: "How was your trip?...Your weather bad up there?...Stay longer in Fort Lauderdale because we are having beautiful weather!...Have a safe trip home!"

We all love Marilyn!

Andy's only other brother Steve is Martin's identical twin. They arrived five minutes apart - Steve first.

Funny, the twin Martin said "Being with my twin brother is like taking a look in the mirror once in a while!"

And, there are quirks about twins.

For two, Martin isn't sure how identical the two are because he claims to be two inches taller than Steve. So it goes.

Anticipation here I come!

Airlines merge in Europe. NASA closes. And Andy says "Hey" instead of "Hi".

Andy joins society whenever and wherever he pleases. Our wedding band must be on his finger or night stand at all times. I tell him that ring is the key to society for us!

Sunday, Father's Day 2010, we have brunch with the Mensa group. His INDUSTRIAL MANUFACTURING COMPANY associates usually come along. They are funny. And oh, yesterday we made whoopie. Midstream I told him "Sayanara" and we had one of the best climaxes ever! This is my Swedish. Andy says that is okay.

Back to an INDUSTRIAL MANUFACTURING COMPANY associate Mike...Does he read Playboy magazine? Last month was a 3D centerfold. His wife Pat is pretty. I wonder.

Andy has a firm hold on a piece of my heart. That heals me. I do highlight tours at the Museum of Art Fort Lauderdale which newly merged with Nova Southeastern University. So.

News flash: Cousin Kathy Herring and husband Mr. David Thiel gave us a baby surprise on June 26, 2010 at over eight pounds! Coincidence? The date is six moonths from Andy's birthday. Do do do do. Another coincidence! Kathy's birthday is six months from her sister Kris's birthday. Do do do do again. Andy has been working hard and over hours. He is a devoted worker. His boss has been going home sick with colds and coughing spells! A third design engineer has been hired named John Miller. We like to talk about cars.

My sister Marilyn gave me a fortune of clothing. And by the way, she is drinking water for a b.m..

I write to Mr. Sven Foss after a ten year letter writing break up. He lives in Oslo and Lofoten Island, Norway. We are friendly but live over three thousand miles away. I guess Andy flirts over the computer. Facebook, email pictures, etc. We are even as I believe it should be.

Life is going on! July 25, 2010. I received a Christmas in July gift. Namely a Toshiba laptop personal computer! Ahhhhh!

Recession bothers me "I suppose" (Andy's words) as I suppose it bothers everyone else. Andy and I have fewer meals out. Andy makes me reassure him that everything under his roof is his. I agree. No choice. I am nothing without him. (!?) Nothing has changed at his employment or he just dsoesn't say. We sold one of his hand made tables and he has temporarily retired from woodworking. Fifty dollars from Maureen Kelley for her daughter Colleen. The table has a small skirt and fancy legs. I called it a King Louie table and it will be going to New Orleans. Now in January 2011 he is returning to the craft of woooworking. Until now, since then, he doesn't show interest in me instead watching pawn shop shows on television before bed. That is the down side.

On the up side we go to Disneyworld to see Mickey and Minnie for cmas. Hooray!

Secretly I need fresh ways to keep Andy interested in our sex life. He has said that is not necessary. That there is something about me he loves that will never change. Immutable. He also said that he likes it best when we are away from home. And so I plan more vacations and hold on tight!

Andy is a very rich man. His family is already counting their inheritance. Ewww. Not a happy reality.

I ponder how much my sister Marilyn talks about me and us. We text message daily. She is Catholic and is for upheaval.

I am a WASP and so is Andy. Be gone with it.

Andy's sister is sick. I sent a plant with balloon for her. No word from her since. For Cmas I sent an electric keyboard to her and she sends us her memoirs with her little girl. All right. Another author after me.

Andy proceeds with green. We planted a solar power driveway from lamps and it looks great. Andy has periodicly rechrged the batteries of some of the lanterns. O/w the sunshine here in Florida suffices for those lanterns. It looks great.

The house has been repainted good for another fifteen years. Pale gray with gray blueish trim. In addition came a flowering tree and silver bushes.

Our northern grass si dying and that is not new. I look for new shrubbage and asked a planter for a Hyacinth bush - the name of an English actress, not a bush - instead of the Honeysuckle bush I want. Tasty yellow flowers. I make mistakes too and I can laugh about it.

Shall I go live in London and leave all of this?

Andy and I recall Britain's King George and we decided he was a survivor because he's homosexual. But why did he talk so much and about what?

Next week, and I mean that with a big German "next", Andy's factory company is showing some of the customers around. Eleven Russian engineers. Hopefully Andy knows what to do and stays clear. Let the management work.

Coincidentaly we found a Russian Market in Boca Raton and were delivered a Russian Life magazine in the post.

Just in case I wrote the hello dobre daynye and goodbye dos vadania on a slip of paper for him. Russians pack alot of fuel. Andy's equipment work in 90% of American power plants. Foreign countries include Korea and India!

...But will he wear the Russian royal plum shirt I bought him for Cmas?

Andy needs his pants mended to 29" inseam. Shall I do that on my 2009 sewing machine? Hopefully not even though I've created clothing for me including seven dresses, jacket and bags...and have a few orders from family. This could be the woman he loves!

1 - 11 -11

Our cars stay good but we save for new ones. Andy is interested in million dollar specialty cars sold in Boca.

Andy's Christmas tree is up and running again going through the den. He called that his responsibility. We accessorized with ho-McDonalds and a fuel station and miniaturized people saying good-bye. Fifteen train cars on a figure eight track. Boys will be boys. Thirty-five billion for a high speed train track in America?

And Andy is back to making furniture now too? I don't know how to slow him down. Thankful we can stop together @ night. Because I have a new breeze passing kiss and an old fashioned Eskimo kiss my daddy taught me as a four year old child....and how am I remembering this hallucination? Freedom from Andy? You better believe it.

Andy is a handy man. Why again now? We needed a toity fix and he did it adjusting leaking screw holds. That is the best description of it I can give.

We are near to Valentives Day. I have expressed to Andy my desire for a red mushy card expressing his passion for us and me. My fingers are crossed.

Andy says he has a new name for me but hasn't told me what it is yet. He works hard now on government specification papers and comes home at about 8pm. I turn him around at the front door and we go out to dinner. That we both like. Good food. Good service. No clean up. Did I say that before? We return and go to bed. Roll up a snow ball and put it between your legs. Ha.

Tomorrow night another party at the Museum of Art. Too, his brother Steve Haber with colleague are showing up for the gala member only event about Vatican Splendors.

I just want to learn from them.

Lately I have discovered the volume of a sphere is close to pi times the radius cubed. Simply thrilling to me. A spatial nirvana!

But how do we measure the volume of a sphere? I suggeast a fillable beach ball and gallon jugs to measure. But where do we get the box? It's all on the computer. Milliliters to inches.

Andy leaves the room and returns with another sphere: a golf ball. Pop pop Fizz fizz he brings out a glass measuring cup half filled with water and now a golf ball too!

And next an ice cube?

Presto! Fudge a little and you know we are right.

The Greeks know more than Grecian Formula hair treatments. Am I right?

Next, I empty the dishwasher and Andy puts a pawn shop show on the tellee. We'll be doing this again!

Andy works late again till 8pm. His boss, who by the way is one year younger than Andy and gets treated like a senior citizen, gives him projects at quitting time and goes home. Andy said he has 60 started projects at work.

I don't worry because this is the year Andy owns his home.

Next maybe huge diamond rings for him? Do we need more payments? Save your money my mother says.

Ungrateful, my mother says.

Sis Marilyn has bronchitis and antibiotics.

My museum of art is showing Vatican art. We have only one picture of Jesus. Byzantine. Otherwise I believe that Jesus is not there. Why? Infant, no. Cruxified? no. His apostle friend Peter holds the keys and apostle Paul keeps a shiny sword. It's very interesting to me. I must bring Andy here.

Andy and I aren't afraid to do different things. For instance, even though we live a block from the supermarket, Andy offers to grow vegetables with me. He wants to put chicken wire over a seed bed! Seeds were too small. I throw out seeds. I needed to see them started somehow.

And we always mull fruit trees in the yard. But why? I can walk across the street and buy perfect fruit at one of the best supermarkets in Florida!

Meanwhile we hear the news of the Tokyo earthquake and power plant disruption. Andy hasn't heard of containing materials for nuclear plants. Beyond water the Japanese need a concrete coverup...in my modest opinion.

And we drift into thought. We discuss WW 2 every once in a while and here we go again. Who were we then if we believe in reincarnation? And today? Are we swayed by our family opinions? Were we people with dogs? Perhaps aristocracy? We see green water at the White House for Saint Pat's. Is this spring or winter I ask?

The price of Japanese cars is up as the nuclear accident grows. And the newspaper shows that on the home front an old man falls off his bike and was killed by a car. Andy reaffirms that he likes cave man wheels!

Andy is thrilled by fake flowers. I buy fourteen pink tulip buds and he says: "Who would?". That is one of our few quotes. I must quote him again!

Winter of 2010 he expressed love for the bird Jesse. THAT PURE AND SIMPLE.

Again screwing is under attack. We now have more to listen for on telle. Already some screwers have been put down as antisocial. Predators are screwy?!? Whew.

This is down time. Andy doesn't feel well. He has inflammation of the shoulder with cramping. Last night he screamed in pain. Oh God. He takes pills so there is a cure. I hate to see him that way. He doesn't even want to hold hands! He has to live. I need him. I cannot live without him.

At this time I seek a new therapist. He is a hoot. Hopefully we can click or jive or whatever. But his first impression of me is that I look schizo. OMG. I want to tell him to look in the mirror too! Haha.

At the regular clinic I hold an appointment with Christine. She is sweet. She says I should speak out because I am a good conversationalist. She makes me feel good.

And back to the real world...Disneyworld again in one week. Andy is feeling better. We will be going for one full week. All four parks.

Andy and I have been having more coincidences. The latest occurred about an ordered computer part. He orders gadgets and a week later the part shows up. I told him he had no package delivery that day and the doorbell rang.

"I'll go check," he says.

Upon opening the front door he was handed his postal gift from the Brown Express mailman.

What?

We laugh here.

Andy is cleaning the backyard pool with a vacuum and algae prevention powder. He says his boy would've watched that from the crib and earn the pool as an adult... Sometimes I put the bird Jesse with him on the pool patio to supervise.

Our yard has four new red hibiscus trees. That is a Florida flower. They were planted for forty-five dollars. Mission blossoming achieved.

Our island of plants is good. A Starlight Chinese bush can be found. A thin palm tree has seen better days but plays a role. Three ivy plants are wilting.

Must buy more flowers.

Andy continues to clean the pool but I get help with service!

On the funner side, Andy and I put a double inflatable mattress in the swimming pool. It was a beautiful day. We were peaceful. We could've slept. Next time a floating beverage holder perhaps. I own four swimsuits. Andy two. I do water aerobics on a noodle float.

NASA closes @ Kennedy Space Center this 2011 year.

"We shall return to outer space with the Russians," Andy wows in a near enough quote.

I must phone my Uncle Don Mooney for another opinion. After all he worked with General Electric in Philadelphia forty years!!!

Uncle Don says Andy is probably right...a continuing spacecraft with missions to Mars and the Moon too.

My thoughts? Please get an interior decorator up there. A blonde buxom woman! Haha. Me!

I figured last year A & I put ten percentage points of our time in top Disneyworld! Four weeks vacation time. We love it!

So far this year 2011 we watched Hurricane Irene speed up the East Coast along with seeing the Titanic movie on t.v. We weren't hit by the storm.

Too, Andy mentioned Marvel comics with 500 dropzons. Will his sci-fi magazine subscription be renewed? Me thinks so.

"Those people forgot to pay their gravity bill!" Andy Haber on August 28, 2011 with Hurricane Irene.

Time passes quietly with that thought, for me anywho. Andy is busy now and here is how I find out:

"Gaget maker...and you have one of them," Andy, September 2011.

And again later a monumental thought: "Bridges are easier to build than computer boards!"

"Not then, not now, not in the future with champagne on the London Eye!"

I muse on returning to London.

"It's possible," I say referring to bubbly on the ferris wheel. Andy: "Look into it."

But that is two years away on our five year plan to London. And without bubbly! Perhaps one beer for me. And no, I am not a lush or lout.

That is part of Andy's reward plan for himself in the future. But, like certain desserts like tiramisu, his favorite, he almost never sees.

2011 and everything in the news is stuff. I notice on my Toshiba laptop that if I ask to follow a certain type of news event e.g. Phillies ballgames or revolutions in Arab countries etc. I can win bronze badges on up.

Questioning Andy's finances, and that could go on forever, Andy says he is closer to being an accountant. Whoh.

I say buying stocks is for people with play money. That draws no response except he lost some money. Could be up to 100,000 dollars. And yes, that is what is in the pocket of a turn of the century American trained and educated engineer!!

Andys latest coincidence, one I could spot, didn't impress him. SAM, Storage and Moving trucks were parked nearby. I spy this one day prior to his meeting with Sam Burton, a friend from woodworking class. What is next?

But, he thinks abstract. At work he now has three symbols as an engineering signature engraved on his products. Products he by the way never sees, uses or finds out about. Wow.

So far, we have 750 pics of us out to dinner with smiles on our faces. In the future we are gonna try no smiles with less posing. Combine that with zooming the pic in and out 3X. And that gave Andy a beautiful screw glow. Me too.

Remember kissing and passing breath air like a last breath in space!!!

Like many others, this is an exciting morning and I get off to a quick start around the house to straighten up. I remove Cmas ornaments from the tree and replace them with Valentine hearts and red-pink garland!

I sort through piles of technical magazines and all kinds of mail. I hope this is good for Andrew. We have bookshelves so I use them, all right?

After that I got my hair cut, trimmed. And it is long and blonde. I asm a savvy woman!

Last night Andy's sister-in-law called on the phone and asked what we are doing. I was amazed because Andy remembered that I brought a transistor radio on our cruise to Haiti and I couldn't pick up any channels on the radio there. That was an early Cmas cruise with Royal Caribbean Cruise Lines Liberty of the Seas. We briefly encountered Labadee, Haiti. Live and learn.

The following day in Falmouth, Jamaica, we picked up twenty or thirty radio channels! We docked at these two ports December 7 and December 8, 2011 respectively.

Aboard ship Andy and I remained sober and active. I remember being questioned by the dining room waiter, "Why white rice?" Onboard, we viewed two 3D movies. We played miniature golf. We posed for pictures now located on our refrigerator door. And I must admit, Andrew and I are a good looking couple!

We are enjoying our beauty by observing a 700 + picture movie on a DVD developed at Walgreens for less than $4! A possible end to 4"x 6" picture photo albums. Me thinks?

Shortly after returning from that cruise, I had an inner ear infection and lung infection. I was treated with pennicillan. How long after one is exposed to germa does one get sick. That was hell.

The Doctor's reason is being exposed to too many people on the cruise ship and not Haiti or Jamaica!!!

I battled that illness for five weeks and yet show signs of a lingering allergy. But what to?

We weren't sick from Tottenham, London or Green Park. There were even gobs of people. And, oh, Springtime, 2011, there were protests there for better living conditions...by the way we plan to return there!

The universe is full of cataclysmic explosive collisions out there.

No one praises our moon for staying put?

We even bomb the South Pole of the Moon? For what?

January 2012 the question is raised: "What is in the Moon?"

Also out there is the comment: "We are brought into the Modern Age because of Rocket Science!" How?

Many colors are fall colors. A crispy brown leaf goes where? Just disintegrating into the breeze?

My sister Marilyn doesn't like pastels (past-tells) we find in the Springtime.

She may change, though, because she wants all colors. The colors of Joseph!

She and Aunt Louise want to go to Italy next year. I doubt it. We see.

And Andy and me? Disneyworld, the Keys and West Palm Beach? Meanwhile we "Have good weekends" along with "Do what is comfortable."

As Cmas approaches Andy brought out his Railroad books...and a miniature train. He has names for the areas of track set out on the den's floor. Santa Fe, Denver etc.

I add miniature houses I collected over two decades. That quiets Andy. That was what I was doing in the past!!?

Flash. Employee beards allowed @ Disneyworld! February 3, 2012.

Well, Andy got a quick view of the Florentine religeous art. Mostly without comment. I was wearing a high culture dress personally sewn and was more interested in the fashioshow at the museum.

Somehow I think the museum goers for that show were more interested in the physical appearance of Christ and the disciples. Perhaps the story behind each picture was cliche or perhaps the patrons to the museum felt uncomfortable in the same light as their Savior. But we can say that we were there, paid our dues and that is final. We were silent. That could be a compliment.

And I come home to fix a meal for us. Then I find out the level of meticulousness Andrew can be. He now owns some of the most expensive and state of the art mills and tools...but he has no electric can opener. Just a rusty little manuel thing I have to ask his help for using! He says six dollars is too expensive! Go figure.

Another awkward way of his behavior comes with the backyard swimming pool. He rarely swims in the pool, maybe once a month, but cleans out the algae and adds chemicals every Sunday! The pool is his cleanliness?

I go to a nearby LAFitness health club on rainy days to swimm. The pool is larger and includes a hot tub jacuzzi and women's only sauna! I save pool toys for Andy's pool including an inflatable double mattress!

February holds the most social engagements for us maybe because many of the Northerners are in Fort Lauderdale during the winter months. Andrew and I meet and dinner date a couple named Tom and Shirley Gleason from Michigan through Boston Mass. We met at a museum party and the guys hit it off about woodworking and we all hit it off about the name Gleason being akin to Carney as in Art Carney of the Honeymooners who is my grand uncle!

Art Carney found his way home to me!

Believe it?

Does my social life equal work?

I am a member never rising.

Does that make me Communistic or just slow or something? What's going on with Andrew?

I clear the dining room table of all his notes and magazines and books and he becomes more quiet. I try and guess his thoughts.

Moon Colony? Aha. Yes!

On a scrap of paper around the house I found a written letter his requesting to NASA to be an astronaut when he was near graduation at his college RPI! And now he has me...a Moonie, Mooney English dissent. What did I walk into here?

My meditation skills are weakening. I light a candle and ponder my English girlfriend Glenyss Jones.

Andy doesn't know how his father and grandfather died so he won't die. This is the modern trend of thought because most fathers are cutting themselves out of family! Fathers are just out there alone somewhere doing fine. Worry for them? That is the dilemma.

Glenyss has an alternative way of the about age, relation and death. Noone knows when they are going to die so the least suspicious is the one who will live forever!

Secretly we all wish to live longer than one hundred years to see what goes on in the course of history. In my opinion too many of us mentally skip over our seventies and eighties and go for the hundred. But twenty years is a long time to sleep!

For my sister Marilyn, my only sibling, I reserve the sixties ands seventies for sisters! Andy and I as a strong couple stays. Hopefully somone will ease Marilyns worries in her sixties. She is a lover, not a fighter!

Glenyss might be a famous Icon where she lives in Oxford, England.

With Glenys in her sixties, she took her eighties mother and 107 year old grandmother to Brighton Beach, England.

Halleliuliah!

And in my own mind I think of yeasterday when Andy and I played with a beach ball catch.

Andy wears a thin sweater of hair. He had his beard and hair cut and left a mass of hair on the floor. Could we do anything with the fur, I wonder?

In addition, his feet are one-quarter million years old. What, you wonder? Small big toe and long toes. When he comes to me to kiss I tell him: "Do not worry, I have human feet!" Ha.

When Andrew comes home from AN INDUSTRIAL MANUFACTURING COMPANY company, he is ready to work. What will it be? Computer room, mechanics room, travel room - any of them could be - or milling room; the garage. What is a mill, you ask. Something like a computerized lathe...

Andy has produced tables, mailboxes, key holders, gavels and pot-per-ie. He has learned how to monogram. And he paints with magic markers and stains wood.

When I am smart I help him with his business. In return he helps me with my dress business.

I've made two dresses, a hat, a jacket and a bag for family. Money trickles in. I like working with specialty cottons and brocades.

Andy works hard at AN INDUSTRIAL MANUFACTURING COMPANY.

He helped Bill come in hired - an engineer who can do math - unlike some of the other applicants. Can you believe thirty divided by one half is sixty? Okay, you qualify. Like me. But some of the so-called engineers failed!!!

Meanwhile, I am back in the tree business! I received a full refund for returning a dead tree less than one year old. The tree lost flowers, didn't grow and was too big for a pot. RIP. That is policy I am gay about.

Oh. I found another advantage being me. Evolutionary height advantage...I can reach to the highest shelf in the supermarket for pasta sauce! Smaller ones must call the manager to get a step ladder. Ha.

Dirty birdie Jesse is good and sings. We have a private choir.

Meanwhile, being part of society, we go to restaurant dinners and brunches with the MENSA group. Three times a month we go to someplace different to be entertained by the service and food!

OK? Of course. I gave Andy money to treat me to dinner and brunch anywhere at my call for the rest of my life.

My creative vow!!!

Guess what? Disney trip soon! Whoopie! Followed by a computer conference in Orlando with a Key Largo topping. Delightful.

Extra special because we have the "Hidden Mickeys" book and shall have extra fun finding the Mickey around the parks!

I am taking new brain medication. It's nothing unusual for the twenty-first century. One forth of our American population does that. They are starting with the kids now!

Except Andy. He has had no prescription pills for stress or anxiety! Mostly after tennis or golfing I give him one or two Tylenol capsules to ease morning after pain...and that is a fight!

See people as walking brains... That is what one doctor said to me.

Andy urinates mid night now. I hope nothing is wrong. One in six men will experience prostate problems. He has had kidney stones removed in 2003! That was scary.

Anyways, a new mind pill I took for two weeks left me depressed, almost incontinent, blurry vision and nautious. I just wanted to get back to what I was before. I complained to the doctor.

Andrew is in the garage now working with the new woodworking mill. He is ambitious and industrious.

He plans to make tables for my friends. The materials cost thousands. We'll see what develops. One year so far.

The bird Jesse is fine. I receive great pleasure seeing the two of them eat dinner simultaneously. For me that is a source of contentment.

During the week Andy comes home to his computer room with numbers in a row. The works work is about linear progressions and one must fill in with mid linear numbers.

At night Andy has a game of Solitaire on the computer before bed.

As a sign of the times, high unemployment and few reources. Marilyn is unemployed again. Andy bears with me.

He increases our house money allowance by forty dollars per month because the cost of food staples rises. 2013 and a gallon of milk costs the same as a gallon of gas for the car!

Today is Sunday and Andy cherishes his peace. He delves into yard work and sweats it out with the heat!

Plans for travel? None right now. Possibly London, England in summertime.

Andrew has perseverence and demands high quality people around him. It is an honor to be around him. He is always doing something. His mind seems clean of thought.

He tolerates no garbage. His motto is: If you stay with and think of the garbage you are garbage!

Needless to say, when household garbage needs to be collected and removed it takes a scant five minutes. Sometimes I forget but that only shows my mind is not on the garbage!?!

Our house has a new bird bath! I've seen robins, blue jays, doves and black birds partake of the water outside the front window. That is truly beautiful.

The birds leave bits of seeds to soften in the water. I try to photograph. Daily, I clean the bird bath. I love those birds!.....and so does Jesse!

Last year I may have made a friend, Jackie C., and last night at dinner she asked me where I grew up...with a smile.

Being prepared to dodge questions about life, I responded: "I haven't finished growing up!"

Ken C. snickered looking down at her. "Pam hasn't stopped growing up..... and with heels she is six feet tallllll!"

Jackie is a cutie.

And Andy and I were there w/o a digital camera! I cannot find my CASIO 10.1 mega pixel camera. Frazzled I search..............Reminded of Prof. Li @ Cornell who hid my mittens three days before returning them to me. That was his game!

My game is that if it was stolen, the camera, the best parts of the camera - cables, instructions and magic cube case - are still with me. A new camera then?

Phoned Glenys and she is up for the London Eye w/ Andy and me 2013. With champagne perhaps?

She commented on my new photography, a "hobby". Until then I didn't know I had a hobby.

Like golf too? Wildlife at the golf course is beautiful. A golf ball in the water and next tens of birds wanting to sit on it! I want my mother!

Meanwhile Andrew works with his mill in the garage! Is he floating away? I was contemplating and criticizing (?) as I was seat-belted into the Honda Accord with Andy @ the wheel.

"What are you gonna do about it?"

I got a strange tingling sensation. I have no answer. Ha.

I am fifty-seven years old and have successfully beaten AHitler who died at fifty-six. I have beaten Captain Morgan who liven to the ripe age of fifty-three! I am two years older than Andy and I am approaching the age twenty-four from a different angle.

Understood? No, I thought so. The reason may go back to Dr. Gavin Rose, my "sickietrist". He links the world as a bunch of dots with an occasional line. It is called Linear thinking and was devised by black Greeks. Yes.

That was a surprise. Dr. Rose gets gummy bear candy for Cmas!

Oh, got a new 88cent can opener (not electric!) for Cmas from Andrew Haber, engineer.

Coincidence is back in our lives...Andrew said he read about someone having a golden labrador retriever dog and what do you know, on our way to a restaurant that night we drove past a man walking a golden lab on Ocean Blvd....a whopping ten miles away! Go figure.

With the Key Largo time share coming up in one week I am reminded of Dr. Rose saying that he would like me to sing like Janis Joplin and presto - from the balcony in Key Largo we could hear from a night club Janis' song being sung!

On the home front, Andy made a request that I make an appointment for screwing with him!

I tried but he fell asleep. I guess he must be relaxing from all of the work he has done...AN INDUSTRIAL MANUFACTURING COMPANY design engineer to crafter of a shelving rack for organizing parts containers.

June 26 has come and gone and he got clothes for his 55 ½ year old birthday!

The date of cuz's Kathy and Dave's daughter's birthday! Another coincidence.

Andy launders shirts and pants to shreds every-other night!

Last week, on a lark, Andrew paid $500 to trim nine olive trees. Presto and done. We look like Sahara desert trees now. And the consequence?

Down came a wonderful blue jay nest with three baby birds. Needless to say....they couldn't survive!

Now, I water more flowers!

September 2013 we need more plans for Disneyworld, Thanksgiving and Cmas.

Kidney stones - more? Hope not. CUPCAKES is the keyword for change the subject!

...I must sew together a cupcake pattern dress. This is the eighth @ the Museum o Art/Fort Lauderdale time that I've worn my creation to a member party!

The price for this is getting high. One hundred dollars for dual membership, sixty dollars to be a docent member and must purchase art books!

Yet, good crowd! 400 guests @ last cocktail/snack party!

And, babies are fine...I send clothes. She is so pretty. Pageant pretty?

Final five contestants in Miss America Pageant are brunette. Winner - Indian New Yorker.

Blondes have a lot of work to do!

Birdie Jesse has East and West houses. He stands on one claw, so proud. He has six ceiling hangings in his big, black cage.

Last month a long, black snake visited me in the laundry room...Andy put on shoes and broomed it out the front door! I think I stepped on it. He was nice.

Halloween is soon to start. Must get Halloween candles. Costumes this year?

My rose tree is in bloom...five dozen red roses. Wow. Need some work done on the north side of house. Artificial plants?

Concordia cruise ship was lifted and towed yesterday, September 18, 2013... cousins Dave and Kathy wedding anniversary. It took 1½ years to move the ship. A human factor to that Italian Titanic is that everyone gets part of the pay out!

My computer is on the dining room table with Andy's. A laptop diversion. A learning tool. A connction to the outer world. Oh, yes, I say to Andy, "I feel like I live in a space capsule!!!"

Needless to say he didn't understand me.

Flash to a high tech breakthrough..a Polaroid digital camera. I know my father would want one.

Andy works on doing a baseball bat...and it works! No cracking yet!

And he tells me that one of his INDUSTRIAL MANUFACTURING COMPANY products was sold to Holland! Yippee, It's a beautiful day 2day.

And Andy sees a doctor check up. His General Practitioner told him to take a pill for diabeties and lose weight he wouldn't call him a diabetic...

A bonus is that he doesn't need glasses!

Socially we are moving back on track. We couple up

And I'm put in a good mood...blue jays have returned to bathe in the bird bath. Along with doves and sparrows!

Shall we plan a trip?

Mid May and yes, April showers brought May flowers.

Andy's health is better from a high tech repair job.

Keeping him off sweets is hard to regulate...but it's do or die!

I keep a three o'clock tea time. My company is Jesse. "Birdie" as Andy calls him. "Birdie" sings as I contemplate plans.

Like what? Home repair, travel, landscaping, fashion, etc.

Andrew want flowers in pots all over the north "lawn" which is sandy dirt topped with black olive leaves...

Dead brown leaves which disintegrate. Who knows where they go to?

Yes, I'm trying to take stock o life now...but it's too ridiculous!

Why? Because it all adds down to chemical composition. I'd rather have a bottle in front o me than a frontal lobotomy. Cool, huh?

And I do think the way to an engineers heart is thru his head!!!

Conclusion: We have very many experiments in our brief but beautiful lives... and I made up another one: What does float a bar o soap? I have the bar o soap (Irish Spring brand); and plenty o water in the back patio pool; Andy and I are gonna see what floats soap for fun?

Answer: Almost any material except thin porous paper material. Go figure!

And the world is still big and wide. What is in store for us? Only the heavens know for sure. A trip home to London perhaps?

Yeah, Andrew and I shall belong to the category of 3% of passengers remaining in Heathrow while everyone else goes to different destinations!!!

G-d is the Power, Kingdom and Glory forever and ever, Amen.

Without an end in sight, I start to look forward to remakes and new movies and the supposed arrival of a holographic telephone 2020!

Dormant for a while, I come out of captivity (hybernation up north) and want to record what I see on camera!

As usual.

A new age of the internet has arrived...Photographs once stuck in my head can be jimmied out and "wowed"!

Making 9,000 + friends on the Internet and the whole world to conquer! Not, of course, to lose track of humble beginnings on a big personal computer and modern set. Laptops have arrived and are here to stay!

...I get personalized world news. Celebrity notifications and personal, social and promotional notes...one of which is bringing Andrew and me to a T-giving dinner party down Miami!

President Barach Obama brings a trillion dollar trade deal to the US with China... All while chewing gum to entice the Russian counterparts... Gum chewing is their symbol equivalent of opening windows... An end to the Cold War with Russia!

President G W Bush unveils his own art work...Magnificent pics of nature plus a portrait of V Putin! (worth?)

And still I volunteer at the Museum of Art Fort Lauderdale still...Accepting guests for an hour long tour. Do we build a clientelle?

Andy is working hard at engineering. He designs computer boards which 40 + concoct, make, assemble.

His kidney stone ultra sound blasting and washing away went pretty well yesterday. We came home to pizza party, him and me. I love him.

Is it Miami's Monkey Jungle the next coming month? Whoah! Or will it be parrot jungle?

Botched supply missions to outer space space stations make us reconsider... Is it worth it???

We try solar power around the house. Not much power!

But, without Florida Power & Light, I manage to solar light a string of LED Christmas lights to adorn the bird cage at night!

And, fianlly an aHa moment is beginning to take shape. Andy thinks I know the proper tea...@ three o'clock in the afternoon with as much snack food I can muster!

And, please, use the most beautiful tea set you have!

The Museum is still pumping!!!

Much status quo... dress making (a new resolution splurge this year) returns to Disney - an adult playground - and a 7+ year old parakeet, a blessing. Living one year with a radio..and 7+ with a telle. Genius or dumb? No figuring.

Andy's model train is out of storage. This new year Andy brings a solar light next to McDonalds and the train track. Crazy. Yet fun!

Good news. Gas prices drop ... meaning more people will be leaving PA. I have a renewed interest in cars...BMW's self parking cars? Funky.

12/31/2010   21:40

The Engagement Party:

Louise Schaible, Marilyn Dixon, Pam Morgan, Andy Haber

The Moon and Pam and Andy

COMMENTS

I got to know them very well. Keep up the good work.

Lenora

It is obvious that love binds you together, you found each other and belong as a pair what would make the story complete is the search that went on prior to your pairing… What made you the person that you are and how did that influence your choice for each other? Perspective is often a story in its own right! May your writing be successful and lighten the path to life's meaning.

Thanks for sharing – so insightful!

Micki

About the Author

Author Pamela Morgan attended University of Pennsylvania and Cornell University. She teaches in an art museum and makes dresses. She lives in Florida with Andrew Haber. Together they travel internationally.

Printed in the United States
By Bookmasters